THE CHEROKEE

A TRUE

by

Andrew Santella

Children's Press®
A Division of Scholastic Inc.

New York Toronto London Auckland Sydney
Mexico City New Delhi Hong Kong
Danbury, Connecticut

A young Cherokee child is dressed in a traditional outfit.

Reading Consultant
Lane Roy Gauthier
*Associate Professor
of Education
University of Houston*

**Visit Children's Press® on
the Internet at:
http://publishing.grolier.com**

Library of Congress Cataloging-in-Publication Data

Santella, Andrew
  The Cherokee / by Andrew Santella
      p. cm. – (A true book)
  Includes bibliographical references and index.
  ISBN 0-516-22216-3 (lib. bdg.)   0-516-27315-9 (pbk.)
  1. Cherokee Indians—History—Juvenile Literature. 2. Cherokee
Indians—Social life and customs—Juvenile Literature. [1. Cherokee
Indians. 2. Indians of North America—Southern States.] I. Title. II. Series.

E99.C5 S36 2001
975.004'9755—dc21   00-031393

GROLIER
PUBLISHING

©2001 Children's Press®,
A Division of Scholastic Inc.

Contents

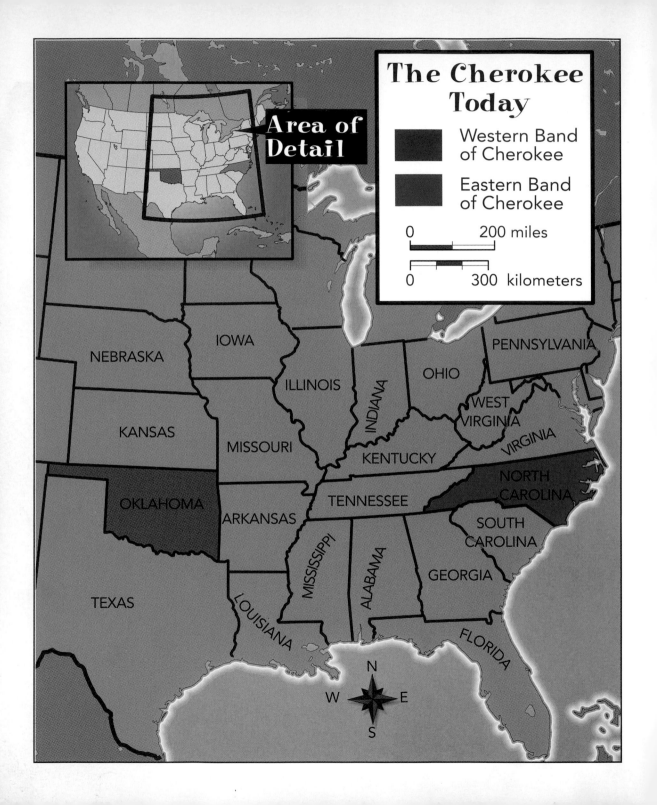

The Cherokee Today

Western Band of Cherokee

Eastern Band of Cherokee

0   200 miles

0   300 kilometers

Area of Detail

NEBRASKA

IOWA

PENNSYLVANIA

ILLINOIS

INDIANA

OHIO

WEST VIRGINIA

KANSAS

MISSOURI

KENTUCKY

VIRGINIA

OKLAHOMA

ARKANSAS

TENNESSEE

NORTH CAROLINA

SOUTH CAROLINA

MISSISSIPPI

ALABAMA

GEORGIA

TEXAS

LOUISIANA

FLORIDA

N
W   E
S

The Real People

The Cherokee are a tribe of American Indians who probably once lived around the Great Lakes in the middle of North America. Hundreds of years ago, these Native Americans moved south and east. They settled in the hills and valleys of what is now the southeastern

United States, where they occupied a vast stretch of land. Their land included parts of what are now Virginia, North Carolina, South Carolina, Kentucky, Tennessee, and Alabama.

They called themselves Ani Yunwiya (ah-nee yun-WE-ya), which means "real people." But their neighbors called them Tciloki (che-LO-kee), which means "people of a different speech." The name Cherokee came from Tciloki.

The Cherokee lived in towns. Each town included about fifty houses and was surrounded by a stockade for protection. A town house, or council house, stood at the center of the town in a large plaza. The town house was a large building made of saplings woven together. In some cases, it could hold as many

A sixteenth century Indian town with stockades surrounding the houses

as 500 people. Its outside walls were plastered with mud, while benches lined the inside walls. In the town house, the Cherokee held community and religious ceremonies.

A town council made important decisions for the people. The council was led by chiefs. Each town could have two chiefs—a red chief and a white chief. Red chiefs led the town in matters of

Ostenaco (left) was a red chief during the 18th century. Cumnacatogue, or Stalking Turkey, (right) was one of three chiefs who traveled to England to meet King George III in 1762.

war. White chiefs upheld the law and handled everyday matters. They also settled arguments between families.

Family Life

The Cherokee lived in two kinds of houses, depending upon the weather. In summer, they lived in large houses made of wood. In winter, they moved into smaller houses called asi (oh-SEE). These were round houses with a pit in the center for fires. A small hole in the top of the roof allowed smoke to escape.

A Cherokee woman usually chose her own husband. After the marriage, the husband lived with his wife's family.

The women planted and took care of the corn, beans, and squash that the Cherokee grew. They also took care of the animals. They prepared all the food and repaired the clothing, too. Some of the women even traveled with Cherokee war parties. They were called war women.

Cherokee men hunted various kinds of animals. They used bows and arrows to hunt bears and deer. To hunt

Arrowheads were used to kill animals.

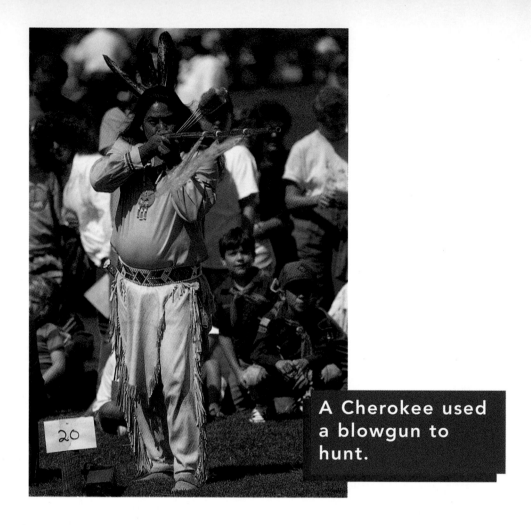

20

A Cherokee used a blowgun to hunt.

small animals, such as rabbits
and squirrels, they shot darts
made of wood and feathers
through blowguns.

The Cherokee used every part of the animal they killed. A bear's hide would become clothing. Its bones might be made into tools, such as knives or needles.

Tools were also made of stone and metal.

This engraving shows how the Cherokee fished.

Bear fat was used as grease, and claws were used as jewelry.

The Cherokee fished in streams and rivers, too. Sometimes they speared fish in the water. Other times they used a hook to catch fish. They also built dams that trapped fish across streams so that they would be easier to catch.

Cherokee Traditions

The Cherokee played a game that was like lacrosse. They called it stickball. The game was played with a stick that had a webbed leather basket on one end. Using the stick, players tried to throw a leather ball into the other team's goal. Games of stickball were often

Stickball was the town sport.

played between two rival towns, with up to fifty men on each team. These games were rough and players were often hurt. The Cherokee called stickball "little brother to war."

The Cherokee had special celebrations to mark the change of the seasons. The most important of these was called the Green Corn Ceremony. It was held when the first corn ripened each summer. According to the Cherokee calendar, this was the start of the new year. At the end of the year, they put out the sacred flame that always burned in the middle of the town. Then the flame was lit again in honor of the new year. The tribal leaders carried torches around the village and lit flames in each house, too.

The new year was a time of new beginnings. Each

A turtle shell rattle was worn during the new year celebrations.

family would clean their house thoroughly and throw away old clothes and tools. Town leaders would forgive all crimes except murder. The celebration continued with a special dance. The women wore rattles made of turtle shells filled with pebbles. As they danced, the shells rattled in time with the music.

Cherokee

Weaving baskets is still a favorite activity.

The Cherokee were skilled at weaving baskets and making pottery. They also made masks used in special dances.

Art

Booger masks were worn during dances.

They were called booger masks and carved from wood and sometimes gourds. Booger masks were supposed to make fun of Cherokee enemies, such as warriors from a rival tribe.

Europeans Arrive

In 1540, a group of Spanish explorers led by Hernando de Soto traveled through the Cherokee lands. It was the Cherokee's first contact with Europeans. Over time, the arrival of Europeans changed everything for the Cherokee. White men brought new

Hernando de Soto stands on the shore of the Mississippi River.

diseases that the Cherokee could not fight off. Between 1715 and 1738, a disease called smallpox killed almost half of the Cherokee people.

Every year more and more Cherokee land was taken over by white settlers.

By the 1800s, missionaries were trying to spread Christianity among the Cherokee. The missionaries tried to teach them to read the Bible in English.

In 1828, the first Cherokee newspaper was started. It was a weekly paper called the *Cherokee Phoenix*. Half of the paper was printed in English and half in Cherokee.

The engraving below shows missionaries having a prayer service. A full-page copy of the *Cherokee Phoenix* from 1828 (right)

The seal of the Cherokee Nation

Around the same time, the Cherokee established a style of government like that of the United States. In 1821, they formed the Cherokee Nation. It was governed by a principal chief, a senate, and a house of representatives. But American settlers still wanted

the Cherokee to move away.
Gold had been discovered on
Cherokee territory in Georgia.
Soon, settlers were pushing
the Cherokee off their land. In
1830, the United States

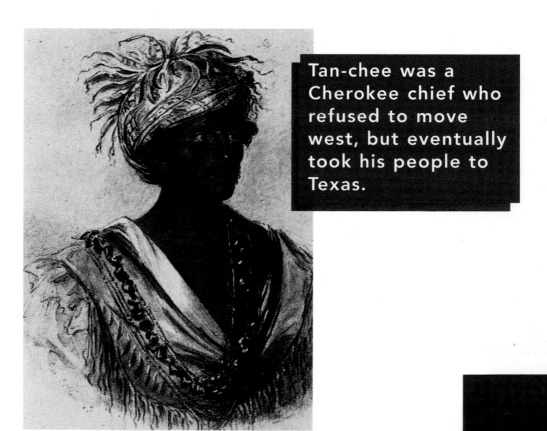

Tan-chee was a Cherokee chief who refused to move west, but eventually took his people to Texas.

passed a law called the Indian Removal Act. That law ordered all Indians to move west of the Mississippi River.

The army began rounding up the Cherokee for the move. Their homes and crops were destroyed, and offices of the *Cherokee Phoenix* were burned down. In 1838, the Cherokee were forced to move west. This forced march became known as the Trail of Tears. Many Cherokee had to walk 800 miles (1,280 km) in

bad weather. They did not have enough food or warm blankets. Four thousand Cherokee died on the way.

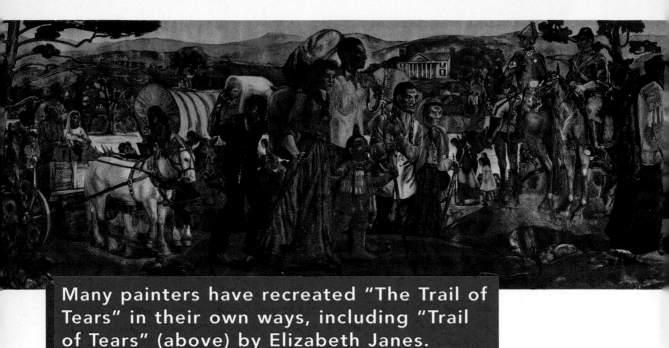

Many painters have recreated "The Trail of Tears" in their own ways, including "Trail of Tears" (above) by Elizabeth Janes.

A few Cherokee hid out in the mountains of North Carolina, but most of them tried to make the move west. Those who survived the Trail of Tears settled in what is now Oklahoma.

Sequoyah and the Syllabary

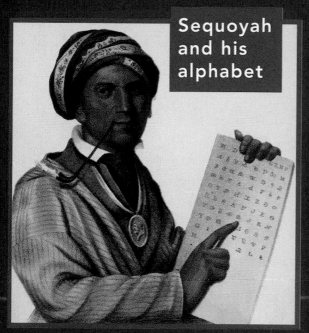

Sequoyah and his alphabet

Sequoyah (1775-1843) was a Cherokee born in Tennessee. He dreamed of inventing a way to write down the Cherokee language. He worked at it for twelve years and finished creating his system in 1821. It consists of eighty-six characters that represent all the sounds in the Cherokee language. The giant sequoia tree and Sequoia National Park in California are named in his honor.

A carved wood statue of Sequoyah on the Cherokee Reservation in Oklahoma

Today's Cherokee

Many Cherokee still live in Oklahoma. They call themselves the Western Band of Cherokee. Most live on land that is owned either by the tribe or by many Cherokee families. The people are governed by a principal chief and a tribal council made up of fifteen members. Each

Today, Cherokee people work in many ways. A man paints a picture of his heritage (above). A woman makes pottery on the reservation (right).

member serves a four-year term. Some Cherokee in Oklahoma work as cattle ranchers. Some raise poultry. Others make and

Jewelry reflects the designs of the past.

sell traditional baskets and pottery for a living. The Cherokee National Museum is in Tahlequah, Oklahoma.

Some Cherokee live in North Carolina. They call themselves the Eastern Band of Cherokee. They are also governed by a

principal chief and a tribal council. The Eastern Band's council is
made up of twelve members
who serve two-year terms. The
tribe owns the Sequoyah Birth-
place Museum in Tennessee.

John Ross was the principal Cherokee chief from 1828-1866.

THE ETERNAL FLAME
THIS FIRE WILL BURN FOREVER AS A SYMBOL
OF FRIENDSHIP ETERNAL BETWEEN THE WHITE
MAN AND THE RED MAN. IT WAS KINDLED WITH
A FLAME FROM A CHEROKEE INDIAN COUNCIL
FIRE THAT HAS BEEN BURNING IN OKLAHOMA
SINCE 1839. THE ORIGINAL FIRE WAS TAKEN TO
OKLAHOMA WHEN ALL BUT A REMNANT OF THE
PROUD CHEROKEE NATION WAS REMOVED WEST
OVER THE INFAMOUS "TRAIL OF TEARS". IN
MAY 1951 FOUR TRIBAL LEADERS FROM THE
QUALLA BOUNDARY, CHEROKEE INDIAN RESER-
VATION, RETRACED THAT TRAIL OF HEART-
BREAK TAKEN BY THEIR ANCESTORS AND
BROUGHT LIVE COALS FROM THE OKLAHOMA
FIRE. THE ETERNAL FLAME HERE AT THE
MOUNTAINSIDE THEATRE WAS KINDLED FROM
THE CENTURY OLD OKLAHOMA FIRE ON JUNE
23, 1951.

PSALM 121:1,2 IN THE CHEROKEE SYLLABARY:

I WILL LIFT UP MINE EYES UNTO THE HILLS, FROM
WHENCE COMETH MY HELP. MY HELP COMETH FROM
THE LORD, WHICH MADE HEAVEN AND EARTH.

The sacred, or eternal, flame continues to burn in Oklahoma.

In 1984, the Western and Eastern Cherokee came together in Tennessee for a reunion. They played a game of stickball, and leaders from each band helped light the sacred flame in honor of the new year.

The Cherokee are the largest Indian tribe in both the United States and Canada today. According to the 1990 census, 308,132 Cherokee live in the United States. Many of them live far from the old tribal lands, but the Cherokee remember their history. Every year, the Cherokee in Oklahoma put on a play

A group of actors perform a scene from *Unto the Hills*.

called *The Trail of Tears*. The Cherokee in North Carolina stage a pageant called *Unto the Hills*. Today, the Cherokee see themselves as a unified people.

Many Cherokee today enjoy getting dressed up like their ancestors to celebrate their heritage.

To Find Out More

Here are some additional resources to help you learn more about the Cherokee:

Books

Claro, Nicole. **The Cherokee Indians.** Chelsea House, 1992.

Fremon, David K. **The Trail of Tears.** New Discovery Books, 1994.

Klausner, Jane. **Sequoyah's Gift.** HarperCollins, 1993.

Lazo, Caroline. **Wilma Mankiller.** Macmillan, 1994.

Lund, Bill. **The Cherokee Indians.** Bridgestone Books, 1997.

Sneve, Virginia Driving Hawk. **The Cherokees.** Holiday House, 1996.

Organizations and Online Sites

Cherokee Heritage Center
http://www.leftmoon.com

Cherokee Nation
http://www.cherokee.org

Cherokee National Museum
http://www.cherokee museum.org

History of the Cherokee
http://pages.tca.net/ martikw

Sequoyah
http://www.powersource. com/gallery/people/ sequoyah.html
A brief biography of the inventor of the Cherokee writing system.

Western Cherokee Nation of Arkansas and Missouri
http://www.western cherokeenation.com

Important Words

blowgun a pipe or tube used to blow darts or other objects

gourd a fruit with a hard shell that is sometimes used to make bottles or bowls

harvest the gathering of crops

lacrosse a ballgame played by two teams. Players use sticks with net pockets to score goals

missionary a person who travels to spread a religious faith

pageant a show in which people act out scenes from history

plaza a public square

rival a person or group competing against another person or group

stockade a wall made of strong wooden posts

Index

Meet the Author

Andrew Santella lives in Chicago, Illinois. He is a graduate of Loyola University, where he studied American literature. He writes for a variety of newspapers and magazines, including the *New York Times Book Review* and *GQ*. He is also the author of several books for young people, including the following Children's Press titles: *The Apache, The Inuit, The Lakota Sioux, The Battle of the Alamo,* and *The Chisholm Trail.*